Duck Stamps

IDENTIFICATION & VALUE GUIDE

L. A. CHAPPELL

COLLECTOR BOOKS
A Division of Schroeder Publishing Co., Inc.

For Bill

Cover design by Beth Summers

Book design by Mary Ann Hudson

COLLECTOR BOOKS
P.O. Box 3009
Paducah, Kentucky 42002-3009

www.collectorbooks.com

Copyright © 2002 L.A. Chappell

All rights reserved. No part of this book may be reproduced, stored in any retrieval system, or transmitted in any form, or by any means including but not limited to electronic, mechanical, photocopy, recording, or otherwise, without the written consent of the author and publisher.

The current values in this book should be used only as a guide. They are not intended to set prices, which vary from one section of the country to another. Auction prices as well as dealer prices vary greatly and are affected by condition as well as demand. Neither the author nor the publisher assumes responsibility for any losses that might be incurred as a result of consulting this guide.

Searching For A Publisher?

We are always looking for people knowledgeable within their fields. If you feel that there is a real need for a book on your collectible subject and have a large comprehensive collection, contact Collector Books.

Contents

Introduction 4
   In the Beginning 4
   At Face Value: The Rising Prices of Stamps 6
   Identification 6
   Selection of the Art 7
   Basic Collecting Questions 8
   Formats for Stamp Collecting 8
   A New Format: Self-Adhesive Issues 9
   Licenses & Covers 10
   Errors 10
   Junior Duck Stamps 10
   Where to Purchase Stamps .11

How to Use This Guide 12

Terminology 13

Stamp-Back Inscriptions 16

Grading System 18

Price Guide & Collector's Log 21

Resources 90

Reference List 92

Introduction

Over the past 70 years, the collecting of United States duck stamps has become quite popular among philatelists, investors, hunters, and conservationists. Consequently, the stamps have increased in value. This book is intended as a reference as well as an inventory log for those with genuine interest in and appreciation of both the stamps themselves and the waterfowl featured on these stamps. Several comprehensive guides and books plus a wealth of information from the U.S. Department of Fish and Wildlife Services documenting the exciting history of duck stamps are available to collectors, but this handy little book will be a great help to beginning collectors, young and old, in addition to the long-time collector. You will find historical information, a photo gallery of all stamp issues, current values, and most essential, a place to keep a record of all your stamps. You will be able to see at a glance just which stamps you have, which you need, and on which ones you can upgrade conditions.

Collectors should exercise caution in selecting duck stamps because, as with all stamps, condition is important. You can add to your collection one stamp at a time or, if you have expendable money, buy a complete set and continue to upgrade.

Today a complete set in very fine, unhinged condition can be purchased for $2,900 to $3,500. We recommend that you educate yourself with the grading system and terms used in the field and purchase stamps only from reputable dealers. Terms for the knowledgeable collector can be found on page 13 of this book.

In the Beginning

The Migratory Bird Hunting Stamp Act was signed by President Franklin D. Roosevelt in 1934, requiring all hunters 16 years of older to buy an annual stamp. Hunters were already required to purchase licenses for hunting privileges, and the stamp served as a receipt for the licensing fees. The Duck Stamp Act, as many call it, was passed due to the efforts of many sincere conservationists concerned about the decrease of wild duck and geese populations partly because of the drainage and disappearance of millions of acres of waterfowl habitat. Overkill and long droughts also contributed to the noticeable decline in waterfowl population.

The first federal duck stamp was issued by the Department of Agriculture. In 1939, the program was passed on to the Department of the Interior and is now managed by the Fish and Wildlife Service (USF&WS).

Introduction

Some states did not require land owners to purchase a license to hunt on their own property, but this policy was changed after just a few years. From 1934 through 1938 after the duck stamp program was enstated, a hunting license was not required for a hunter on his own property. The United States Postal Service (USPS) issued a green Form 3333 to which these hunters attached their duck stamps. The stamp was required, even though the actual license was not. A Form 3333 in better condition with the stamps attached commands high prices with collectors and dealers.

Almost all the funds generated by sale of the federal duck stamps are used to purchase land for the 94-million-acre National Wildlife Refuge system as well as to secure easements on private land. Since the inception of the program in 1934, sales of duck stamps have raised over $500 million to purchase over 5 million acres of wetlands and other wildlife habitat. The Department of the Interior has also helped to secure other government funding to amend these efforts.

Duck stamp monies have also been used to develop and maintain the refuge land, to enforce the duck stamp laws, and to produce and distribute the stamps.

After purchase by a hunter, duck stamps must be validated by the purchaser by signing in ink his or her name. Many issues of the early stamps were not signed because hunters were not accustomed to such a practice. Most stamps were slipped into wallets for safekeeping and forgotten until time to purchase the next year's stamp. Used, unsigned copies of these earlier issues can be found quite frequently. Your best resource is the creditable dealers on the Internet and those still issuing regular mail-order stamp catalogs. There are a number of good publications for the collector as well as a vast resource on the Internet (see Resources on page 90).

Often the early issues of the stamps bear complete postmarks of the city, state, and date of purchase. Known to collectors as "socked on the nose" (SOTN), these stamps command a premium value in the field.

Prior to issue #20, duck stamps were printed on ungummed paper that had been dampened. Natural bends are to be expected and are not considered defects. Dry, gummed paper has been used since issue #21, and stamps through the current issue #69 should be free of gum bends, skips, etc.

The flat plate, one-color printing process was used from issue #1 through issue #25. The two-plate rotary (Giori) press, first used with issue #26, allowed multicolor stamps.

The USF&WS still heads the Federal Duck Stamp Program through its Federal Duck Stamp office. The rising cost of wetlands has forced the need to increase the cost of the stamps periodically throughout the program's history.

Introduction

At Face Value:
The Rising Prices of Stamps

Remarkably, the issue price of the federal stamp remained at $1 for 15 years. Prices have climbed to the current face vaue of $15 due to the rising cost of land and expansion of the Federal Duck Stamp Program. The chart below gives a quick glance at how much and when the face value has increased. A complete set of stamps, purchased at face value each year at the time of issue, over the years would have cost $369. Today that complete set, issues #1 through #68, could be worth anywhere from $2,800 in Fine condition to roughly $9,500 in Very Fine+ condition – quite a worthwhile investment.

Years	Issue Price
1934 – 1948	$1.00
1949 – 1958	$2.00
1959 – 1971	$3.00
1972 – 1978	$5.00
1979 – 1986	$7.50
1987 – 1988	$10.00
1989 – 1990	$12.50
1991 – present	$15.00

Identification

Including the stamp issued for the year 2001, there are 68 stamps available to collectors. Rather than classifying them by their year of issue, using a standard system recognized by other collectors is helpful. The most often used system for all stamps is from the Scott Catalog Company. For duck stamps, this system uses the letters RW (Revenue Waterfowl) followed by the series number, e.g., RW1 is the first federal duck stamp, issued in 1934. Stamps are numbered consecutively by year from 1934. An alternate system was designed by the Krause-Minkus Standard Catalog of U.S. Stamps which also uses a number system with the letters RH (Revenue Hunting). We have chosen to simply number the stamps in their order of issue (#1 through #68) along with the year during which it was valid. Stamps are issued for a one-year period of which the "void

Introduction

after" date printed on the face is the end. They are actually printed in and sales begin at the end of the year before the void after year. The first stamp, our #1 on page 22, was issued for the year 1934 – 1935 and is known both as the 1934 and the 1934 – 1935 issue. A quick method for figuring a stamp's issue number is to subtract 1934 from the "void after" year; if the void after year is 1966, subtract 1934 to determine that the stamp is issue #32.

Selection of the Art

The art for the very first federal duck stamp was designed by Jay N. "Ding" Darling at President Franklin D. Roosevelt's request. Darling, a well-known political cartoonist, was also an avid hunter and conservationist and had been instrumental in the development of the duck stamp program. In the following years, nationally known wildlife artists were asked to submit their designs for selection. The first open competition for the stamp art was in 1949.

Each year since 1950, the art for the next stamp is selected from a contest open to all interested artists. Judging is done each year by a group of art, stamp, and waterfowl experts appointed by the Secretary of the Interior, and popularity of this contest seems to grow every year. The website of the USF&WS in the Department of the Interior (http://duckstamps.fws.gov) sees an extraordinary increase in traffic near the time of the announcement of the winner around the end of October.

This contest is the only federally-sponsored art competition. The winning artist receives a pane of the stamps and retains copyright to the original artwork, so he or she can still sell limited edition prints of the work. Several contest winners have earned as much as $1 million in royalties on such prints.

The 2002 federal stamp contest, issue #69, was won by Joseph Hautman for his acrylic painting of a black scoter, winning over 245 other artists in the annual competition. Joe also won the 1992 contest and his brothers, Bob and Jim, have won this contest several times. The new stamp will go on sale July 1, 2002, and will be valid through June 30, 2003.

Acrylic painting of black scoters by Joe Hautman to be featured on the 2002 – 2003 stamp (#69).

Introduction

Basic Collecting Questions

Collecting duck stamps is a fun hobby. Most collectors are either hunters and/or conservationists, but anyone can appreciate the beautiful art on these stamps. As with any collection, one must first decide what the goal and budget will be – do you wish to obtain an entire set of singles in mint condition? Do you want to frame and display them? Do you have a limited budget or is price no object? Many collectors specialize by collecting stamps on licenses, artist-signed stamps, plate blocks, used stamps (ones signed by the hunters), souvenir cards, art prints, or first-day covers.

Every U.S. state has also issued duck stamps as well as have many tribal organizations and numerous foreign countries. These can become sideline collections after you've acquired the entire set of singles of the federal stamps.

As you can see, there is virtually no limit to the items to collect or the fun, except possible restrictions from your budget.

Formats for Stamp Collecting

The different formats for collecting federal duck stamps, such as mint or used singles, plate singles or blocks, and errors, are what make collecting exciting.

As singles, the stamps are collected both unused and used. Since some hunters didn't actually sign their stamps, there are also two categories of used stamps: signed and unsigned.

Any stamp appearing mint on the face but without gum was probably soaked or steamed off a license by either the hunter or a stamp collector. Artist-signed stamps are another format; the artist will sign either the stamp face or the attached selvage.

Single stamps are subject to the same grading conditions as any other collectible stamps.

The federal stamps have all been printed by the Bureau of Engraving and Printing (BEP) and issued in panes of various sizes with plate numbers. Duck stamps are printed in large sheets that are then cut into panes.

Through 1958, duck stamps were printed in 112-stamp sheets that were cut into 28-stamp panes. The plate number was printed above or below the second stamp in from the corners on top and bottom. These plate numbers them-

Introduction

selves are collectible as plate singles and blocks. These early issues are collected as plate blocks of six, with full selvage on two adjacent sides and a vertical pair of stamps to the right and left of the pair with the plate number.

In 1959 the sheet format was changed to 120 stamps, which were quartered into panes of 30 stamps. In addition, the plate number was moved to the side of the corner stamps. These issues are collected as corner plate singles (with all selvage) and as blocks of four. The 1964 stamp is an exception because the plate number was mistakenly placed in the former position. In 2000, the sheet format was changed to 80 stamps, then divided into 20-stamp panes. Plate numbers were printed on all four corners to accommodate the demand by collectors for plate singles and blocks.

Since 1998 the duck stamp has also been printed in a single-stamp self-adhesive format (see below). It is likely that this will be the preferred format for sales to hunters. The sheet format will be continued, mainly for collectors, for sale through the USPS Philatelic Service.

A New Format: Self-Adhesive Issues

The USF&WS introduced the self-adhesive federal duck stamp single for a three-year trial run beginning in 1998, in response to the many stamp distributors' requests for a single-stamp format which would be easier to handle. These issues make attractive additions to a collection. The service will surely continue the production of these self-adhesives.

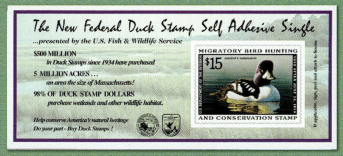

1998 Issue #65SA

Introduction

Licenses & Covers

Postal collectors actively seek first-day covers (FDC) which are envelopes with the newly released stamps affixed and conceled on that first day of issue stamps on covers and value the cancellations and markings. For duck stamp collectors, the equivalent of a cover is a hunter-signed stamp on a license. Collecting a full set of duck stamps on licenses is much more challenging than collecting a set of stamp singles. Assembling a full set of duck stamps on licenses from just your home state is even more challenging, as is collecting a license from every state, but specialty collecting is what makes collecting exciting.

In 1934, not every state required hunting licenses. For these areas, the federal government issued a special form, Form 3333, that contained a place for the stamp to be affixed and spaces for the hunter to sign and have validated by a postmark. Complete validated forms currently sell for premium prices.

Some serious collectors even created "first-day covers" (FDC) of duck stamps by affixing a duck stamp and a current postage stamp to an envelope and having both canceled on the day the duck stamp was issued. Special covers and cancelations have been offered by the USPS at first-day ceremonies for the duck stamps.

Errors

Printing errors are fairly uncommon for federal duck stamps though color omissions or shifts, plate flaws, paper folds, and inversions and omissions of the back inscriptions exist for some issues. As with postage stamps, these flawed stamps are highly sought after and often command unusually high prices. When buying or trading these types of stamps, be sure to work with a reputable dealer.

Junior Duck Stamps

The Junior Duck Stamp Program is an educational and development program for young wildlife artists which has grown rapidly since it was begun in 1989.

State and national art competitions are held each year for the design of a Junior Duck Stamp. In 1992, the USF&WS issued 5,000 souvenir sheets which sold for $10 each, showing nine winning pieces of art from state competitions held during 1991 and 1992. Since 1993, a single $5 stamp displaying the winning artwork has been issued. These stamps are collectibles but are not valid for any hunting purpose and make an attractive and inexpensive addition to any duck stamp collection. These young hunters, stamp collectors, and artists will help promote and strengthen the tradition of the duck stamp program as well as wetlands preservation.

Introduction

Where to Purchase Stamps

Federal duck stamps may be purchased directly from the Federal Duck Stamp office in Washington, D.C., most wildlife refuge offices, any first or second class U.S. post office, plus many sporting goods stores.

Go early, soon after the new stamp's release on July 1, to purchase the new issue each year. The selection will be better, and the retailers will most likely allow you time to find the best possible stamp available. Many larger U.S. post offices have philatelic windows, and the clerks are very helpful to collectors.

Older issues of duck stamps can be purchased from other hunters or stamp collectors, stamp auctions or dealers.

Make your friends and fellow hunters aware of your collection. Often hunters who are not collectors keep their stamps over the years and often have their fathers' as well. Many great stamps have been obtained from such local discoveries. There are many other ways to collect on the local level, such as through stamp clubs and shows or classified ads. This process is slow since the supply is very limited – the chance of your finding someone willing to sell exactly what you need is very slim.

Due to the ever-expanding Internet, the collecting process has become global. There are numerous sites available to collectors on the web – auction houses, retail stamp dealers, plus many sites devoted exclusively to duck stamps. See Resources, page 90, for some recommended websites.

The most popular source for duck stamps is mail order. A number of dealers specializing in duck stamps provide better selection and service. We recommend using these reputable dealers when purchasing the older, more expensive issues. Most dealers have websites as well as mail-order catalogs which can prove very informative to collectors. These dealers will most likely allow you to return any stamps if not completely satisfied.

It is important when building a collection to also build relationships with just one or two primary dealers. This not only requires patience, trust, and respect, but it also creates a good source for information, advice, and of course, stamps.

How to Use This Guide

This handy little reference and value guide can aid collectors in obtaining and maintaining their collections. As with any collectible, the collector is wise to become informed and educated in his field. Several comprehensive books on the market delve into the exciting history of the Federal Duck Stamp program. This guide is designed to be carried with you and used as an inventory and checklist.

Once you have read the brief Introduction, review the price guide beginning on page 21. Every stamp is featured in full color, making quick identification possible. Included on each page is the specific information any collector or dealer would require: the artist, the species featured, the plate numbers, and designers, even the exact wording found on both the front and the back of each stamp.

These values reflect the ever-changing market. Values were established by averaging prices from reputable dealer catalog lists, recent realized auction prices, and Internet stamp retailers. We also incorporated prices from duck stamp dealers and general postage stamp dealers. This average gives the collector a good range of values. And again, we must stress that this is only a guide. You as the collector must personally decide the prices you are willing to pay in order to obtain the stamps needed to complete your collection.

As with any stamp issue, there are grades and conditions which directly affect the value. Values are given for varying conditions; you will find a space below each value/condition in which you can mark your inventory, filling in the prices you paid to obtain each stamp.

In addition to this main section, you will find the Reference List on pages 92 – 95. This can be used as a quick reference as well as an index to this book. Preceding each stamp listing is a check box. As you acquire your stamps, simply mark them in your inventory. Carry this book with you to shows and shops, and see your inventory at a quick glance.

Terminology

AS (artist signed): A stamp which has been signed or autographed on the face of the stamp by the artist who created the artwork. These signed stamps are gaining in popularity and are commanding premium prices, especially those signed by artists now deceased.

Certificates of appreciation: Since 1960, the USF&WS has issued Certificates of Appreciation and souvenir cards that were given with the purchase of a duck stamp. These provided space where the stamp could be affixed and canceled with regular postage.

Condition: Condition is extremely important to all stamp collectors. Factors to consider are sharpness of the perforations, centering of the overall printing, and brightness of color and design. Value is assessed based on condition as much as rarity. Stamps that show any damage such as stains, creases, tears, or thinned spots are priced considerably lower due to these conditions.

FDC (first-day cover): The FDC is usually an envelope or card on which the new stamp is affixed for cancellation on the date of issue. Since the duck stamp is not legal postage, a postage stamp is also affixed to a card or envelope before the postmark is stamped. Often a special commemoration or event is held upon the release or introduction of a new stamp in Washington, DC.

Form 3333: From 1934 through 1938, in some states a hunting license was not required if a hunter was on his own property. The USPS issued a green Form 3333 where these hunters could attach their duck stamps. The stamp was required, even though the actual license was not. These early forms in better condition with the stamps attached command high prices with collectors and dealers.

Grading: A system to aid in assessing values which is based mainly on the centering of the overall design on the face of the stamp (see also Grading System on page 18).

Gum: The adhesive material on backs of stamps. Creases and bends in the gum on early issues are merely a result of the production process and do not detract from the stamp's value or collectibility.

Terminology

Hinged: A stamp having original gum but also possessing a small mark on the gum from a peelable glassine hinge that once held the stamp in a collector's album. Many dealers and collectors further break down this condition to "light hinged" (LH) or "heavy hinged" (HH). Often the hinge mark can be seen through the front of the stamp which greatly reduces value.

Issue date: Federal duck stamps are issued on July 1 and expire June 30 the following year. The "void after" date is always printed on the face of the stamp.

Mint: A stamp in the exact condition as when purchased at time of issue.

NH (never hinged): A stamp that has never had a glassine hinge attached to it.

Perforations: The evenly spaced series of holes around the outside edges of the stamps which allow the stamps to be separated into strips or singles.

Plate block (PB): A group/set of four or six duck stamps with the plate number still attached in the selvage of the stamp sheet. All perforations are left intact. All plate blocks are mint, never hinged, with original gum. Issues #1 – #25 and #31 are plate blocks of six; all others are plate blocks of four stamps.

Plate single: A single stamp containing a plate number on its selvage. For value on issues #1 – #50, add 15% to mint price. For issues #51 – current, add 10% to mint price.

Postmark: Many early stamp issues were canceled by the postal service. This mark included a circular hand-stamped mark with the hunter's local city, state, and date of purchase. Used stamps with a centered and clear cancellation, known by collectors as "socked on the nose," are priced at full used collector values.

Premium used: A used stamp that has only a light signature and is in sound condition.

Prints: All winning duck stamp designs have been reproduced as limited edition art prints. The beautiful artwork is showcased in high quality printing. The early editions are black and white prints which were released in very limited numbers. Exercise great caution since fakes of many issues do exist. Buy from reputable dealers. The prints make excellent investments and exciting additions to your stamp collection.

Terminology

RH (Revenue Hunting): Prefix of the Krause-Minkus Catalog numbering system for duck stamps used by many collectors and dealers.

RW (Revenue Waterfowl): Prefix of the Scott Catalog numbering system for duck stamps.

Straight edge (SE): Many early stamps can be found with one or two borders without any perforations. Most dealers usually deduct 10% to 20% from the vaue of stamps with straight edges. The outer borders of the early 28-stamp sheets were not perforated. Consequently, early issues of these stamps (issues #1 – #12) with all four sides perforated command a high premium among collectors and dealers. Straight edges did not occur on issues after #12.

Unsigned (Unsgnd): A stamp affixed to a license but not signed by the hunter. Keep in mind that the hunter may have used the stamp, carrying it in his wallet for the season, and was either unaware that the signature was required for validation or just never took the time to sign it.

Used: A stamp signed by the duck hunter. It is recommended that the hunter sign his or her name very small in a spot on the stamp which is not part of the main design. It is better to sign up one side of the background or border rather than straight across the front as many hunters did in the past.

Stamp-Back Inscriptions

Issues from 1934 through 1945 did not have inscriptions on the back of the stamp.

Beginning in 1946, an inscription was printed directly on the paper under the gum. In 1954 the message was then printed on top of the gum.

IT IS UNLAWFUL TO HUNT WATERFOWL UNLESS YOU SIGN YOUR NAME IN INK ON THE FACE OF THIS STAMP.

1946 – 1953 (#13 – #20) Message printed on stamp under gum.
1954 – 1958 (#21 – #25) Same message printed on top of gum.

DUCK STAMP DOLLARS BUY WETLANDS TO PERPETUATE WATERFOWL.
IT IS UNLAWFUL TO HUNT WATERFOWL UNLESS YOU SIGN YOUR NAME IN INK ON THE FACE OF THIS STAMP.

1959 – 1960 (#26 – #27). 1959 was inverted.

DUCK STAMP DOLLARS BUY WETLANDS FOR WATERFOWL.
IT IS UNLAWFUL TO HUNT WATERFOWL UNLESS YOU SIGN YOUR NAME IN INK ON THE FACE OF THIS STAMP.

1961 – 1967 (#28 – #34).

BUY DUCK STAMPS SAVE WETLANDS
SEND IN ALL BIRD BANDS
SIGN YOUR DUCK STAMP

1968 – 1969 (#35 – #36).

Stamp-back Inscriptions

**BUY DUCK STAMPS
SAVE WETLANDS**

SEND IN *ALL* BIRD BANDS

SIGN YOUR DUCK STAMP

IT IS UNLAWFUL TO HUNT WATERFOWL UNLESS YOU SIGN YOUR NAME IN INK ON THE FACE OF THIS STAMP

1970 – 1986 (#37 – #53).

**TAKE PRIDE IN AMERICA
BUY DUCK STAMPS
SAVE WETLANDS**

SEND IN ALL BIRD BANDS

SIGN YOUR DUCK STAMPS

IT IS UNLAWFUL TO HUNT WATERFOWL UNLESS YOU SIGN YOUR NAME IN INK ON THE FACE OF THIS STAMP

1987 – 1989 (#54 – #56).

**TAKE PRIDE IN AMERICA
BUY DUCK STAMPS
SAVE WETLANDS**

SEND IN ALL BIRD BANDS

SIGN YOUR DUCK STAMPS

IT IS UNLAWFUL TO HUNT WATERFOWL OR USE THIS STAMP AS A NATIONAL WILDLIFE ENTRANCE PASS UNLESS YOU SIGN YOUR NAME IN INK ON THE FACE OF THIS STAMP

1990 (#57).

**TAKE PRIDE IN AMERICA
BUY DUCK STAMPS
SAVE WETLANDS**

SEND IN ALL BIRD BANDS

IT IS UNLAWFUL TO HUNT WATERFOWL OR USE THIS STAMP AS A PASS TO A NATIONAL WILDLIFE REFUGE UNLESS YOU SIGN YOUR NAME IN INK ON THE FACE OF THIS STAMP.

1991 – 1992 (#58 – #59).

**TAKE PRIDE IN AMERICA
BUY DUCK STAMPS
SAVE WETLANDS**

SEND IN ALL BIRD BANDS

IT IS UNLAWFUL TO HUNT WATERFOWL OR USE THIS STAMP AS A PASS TO A NATIONAL WILDLIFE REFUGE UNLESS YOU SIGN YOUR NAME IN INK ON THE FACE OF THIS STAMP

1993 (#60).

**INVEST IN AMERICA'S FUTURE
BUY DUCK STAMPS
SAVE WETLANDS**

SEND IN ALL BIRD BANDS

IT IS UNLAWFUL TO HUNT WATERFOWL OR USE THIS STAMP AS A PASS TO A NATIONAL WILDLIFE REFUGE UNLESS YOU SIGN YOUR NAME IN INK ON THE FACE OF THIS STAMP.

1994 – 1996 (#61 – #63).

**INVEST IN AMERICA'S FUTURE
BUY DUCK STAMPS AND
SAVE WETLANDS**

**SEND IN OR REPORT ALL
BIRD BANDS TO
1-800-327-BAND**

IT IS UNLAWFUL TO HUNT WATERFOWL OR USE THIS STAMP AS A PASS TO A NATIONAL WILDLIFE REFUGE UNLESS YOU SIGN YOUR NAME IN INK ON THE FACE OF THIS STAMP.

1997 – present (#64 – #68).

Grading System

As with most collectibles, condition is of the utmost importance when evaluating duck stamps and assessing values. A sound grading system is one based mainly on the centering of the overall design on the face of the stamp. Perfectly centered, extremely fine condition stamps are valued substantially more than those with average or normal centering. It is difficult to find duck stamps which are perfectly centered. The norm is Very Fine in stamp collecting; you should familiarize yourself with all of the following terms regarding condition and collecting of stamps in general. The more knowledgeable you are, the better your collection will be, and you will be able to buy, sell, or trade with confidence.

Mint: Seldom found, these stamps are perfectly centered and in the same condition as when purchased after printing. High values are to be expected for these superb stamps.

Extremely Fine (XF): A stamp with nearly perfect centering. Collectors will pay a premium price for XF stamps because they are so difficult to find.

Very Fine (VF): A stamp that is nearly perfectly centered. The design may be off a bit on one side.

Fine (F): A stamp in which perforations clear the design although they may be close. The design is off-center on one or more sides.

Average (AVG): A stamp which may contain minor faults such as short perforations, creases, or have poor centering so perforations cut into the design.

Poor: Stamps with major faults such as tears or scrapes are 50% of the value of average stamps. These stamps are good for starting collections and are occasionally acceptable for framing but are the lowest acceptable grade for collectors.

Grading System

Two examples showing varying degree of centering.

Grading System

#39 single showing selvage and plate number.

#2 single showing inperforate left edge.

Price Guide & Collector's Log

Price Guide & Collector's Log

1934 – 1935 **#1**
Mallards
Artist: Jay N. "Ding" Darling

Front: "U.S. Department of Agriculture. Void After June 30, 1935. Migratory Bird Hunting Stamp. 1, One Dollar"
Plates Issued: 129199, 129200, 129201, 129202
Designer: Alvin R. Meissner
1st Day of Sale: August 22, 1934
Qty. Sold: 635,001

Used			*Unsigned*			*Mint*		
AVG.	F	VF	NH F	NH VF	NH XF	H F	NH F	NH VF
$45	$95	$140	$70	$140	$160	$260	$420	$675

Price Guide & Collector's Log

1935 – 1936   #2
Canvasbacks
Artist: Frank W. Benson

Front: "U.S. Department of Agriculture. Void After June 30, 1936. Migratory Bird Hunting Stamp. 1 Dollar."
Plates Issued: 131980, 131981, 131982, 131983
Designer: Alvin R. Meissner
1st Day of Sale: July 1, 1935
Qty. Sold: 448,204

Used			*Unsigned*			*Mint*		
AVG.	F	VF	NH F	NH VF	NH XF	H F	NH F	NH VF
$60	$100	$145	$115	$175	$200	$235	$395	$650

23

Price Guide & Collector's Log

1936 – 1937 #3
Canada Geese
Artist: Richard E. Bishop

Front: "U.S. Department of Agriculture. Void After June 30, 1937. Migratory Bird Hunting Stamp. 1 Dollar."
Plates Issued: 131980, 131981, 131982, 131983
Designer: Richard Bishop
1st Day of Sale: July 1, 1936
Qty Sold: 448,204

Used			Unsigned			Mint		
AVG.	F	VF	NH F	NH VF	NH XF	H F	NH F	NH VF
$30	$65	$75	$45	$95	$100	$135	$195	$295

Price Guide & Collector's Log

1937 – 1938   **#4**
Greater Scaups
Artist: Joseph D. Knap

Front: "U.S. Department of Agriculture. Void After June 30, 1938. Migratory Bird Hunting Stamp. 1 Dollar."
Plates Issued: 136267
Designer: Alvin R. Meissner
1st Day of Sale: July 1, 1937
Qty. Sold: 783,039

Used			Unsigned			Mint		
AVG.	F	VF	NH F	NH VF	NH XF	H F	NH F	NH VF
$10	$45	$50	$25	$65	$85	$115	$175	$250

Price Guide & Collector's Log

First issue to sell over one million stamps.

1938 – 1939   #5
Northern Pintails
Artist: Roland H. Clark

Front: "U.S. Department of Agriculture. Void After June 30, 1939. Migratory Bird Hunting Stamp. 1 Dollar."
Plates Issued: 138602
Designer: Alvin R. Meissner
1st Day of Sale: July 1, 1938
Qty. Sold: 1,002,715

Used			Unsigned			Mint		
AVG.	F	VF	NH F	NH VF	NH XF	H F	NH F	NH VF
$10	$45	$50	$28	$65	$85	$125	$175	$325

Price Guide & Collector's Log

1939 – 1940
Green-Winged Teal
Artist: Lynn Bogue Hunt

#6

Front: "Void After June 30, 1940. Migratory Bird Hunting Stamp. U.S. Department of the Interior. 1 Dollar."
Plates Issued: 141428
Designer: William K. Schrage
1st Day of Sale: July 1, 1939
Qty. Sold: 1,111,561

Used			Unsigned			Mint		
AVG.	F	VF	NH F	NH VF	NH XF	H F	NH F	NH VF
$10	$30	$40	$20	$45	$60	$75	$125	$195

27

Price Guide & Collector's Log

1940 – 1941 **#7**
Black Ducks
Artist: Francis L. Jacques

Front: "Void After June 30, 1941. $1. Migratory Bird Hunting Stamp. U.S. Department of the Interior."
Plates Issued: 143743, 143776
Designer: Victor S. McCloskey, Jr.
1st Day of Sale: July 1, 1940
Qty. Sold: 1,260,810

Used			Unsigned			Mint		
AVG.	F	VF	NH F	NH VF	NH XF	H F	NH F	NH VF
$10	$30	$35	$20	$45	$60	$75	$125	$195

Price Guide & Collector's Log

1941 – 1942
Ruddy Ducks
Artist: Edwin R. Kalmbach

#8

Front: "Void After June 30, 1942. Migratory Bird Hunting Stamp. U.S. Department of the Interior. $1."
Plates Issued: 146271, 146282
Designer: Victor S. McCloskey, Jr.
1st Day of Sale: July 1, 1941
Qty. Sold: 1,439,967

Used

AVG.	F	VF
$10	$30	$35

Unsigned

NH F	NH VF	NH XF
$20	$45	$60

Mint

H F	NH F	NH VF
$75	$120	$195

Price Guide & Collector's Log

1942 – 1943 **#9**
American Wigeons
Artist: Alden Lassel Ripley

Front: "Void After June 30, 1943. Migratory Bird Hunting Stamp. U.S. Department of the Interior. 1 Dollar."
Plates Issued: 149599, 149600
Designer: William K. Schrage
1st Day of Sale: July 1, 1942
Qty. Sold: 1,383,629

Used			Unsigned			Mint		
AVG.	F	VF	NH F	NH VF	NH XF	H F	NH F	NH VF
$15	$30	$40	$25	$50	$65	$75	$125	$195

Price Guide & Collector's Log

1943 – 1944
Wood Ducks
Artist: Walter E. Bohl

#10

Front: "U.S. Department of the Interior. Void After June 30, 1944. Migratory Bird Hunting Stamp. $1."
Plates Issued: 152826, 152827
Designer: Victor S. McCloskey, Jr.
1st Day of Sale: July 1, 1943
Qty. Sold: 1,169,352

Used			*Unsigned*			*Mint*		
AVG.	F	VF	NH F	NH VF	NH XF	H F	NH F	NH VF
$15	$30	$35	$25	$35	$40	$45	$50	$75

Price Guide & Collector's Log

1944 – 1945 **#11**
White-Fronted Geese
Artist: Walter A. Weber

Front: "U.S. Department of the Interior. Void After June 30, 1945. Migratory Bird Hunting Stamp. $1."
Plates Issued: 155590, 155603
Designer: William K. Schrage
1st Day of Sale: July 1, 1944
Qty. Sold: 1,487,029

Used

AVG.	F	VF
$10	$20	$25

Unsigned

NH F	NH VF	NH XF
$18	$30	$35

Mint

H F	NH F	NH VF
$45	$60	$90

32

Price Guide & Collector's Log

1945 – 1946   **#12**
Northern Shovelers
Artist: Owen J. Gromme

Front: "Void After June 30, 1946. Migratory Bird Hunting Stamp. U.S. Department of the Interior. $1."
Plates Issued: 157248, 157249
Designer: Victor S. McCloskey, Jr.
1st Day of Sale: July 1, 1945
Qty. Sold: 1,725,505

Used			Unsigned			Mint		
AVG.	F	VF	NH F	NH VF	NH XF	H F	NH F	NH VF
$6	$18	$20	$12	$28	$30	$32	$35	$65

Price Guide & Collector's Log

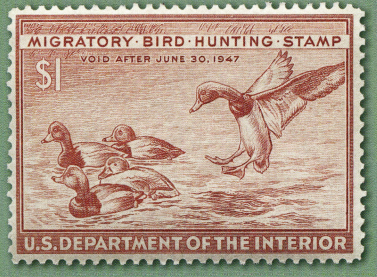

First stamp with printing on the back.
First issue to sell over two million stamps.

1946 – 1947
Redheads
Artist: Bob Hines

#13

Front: "Migratory Bird Hunting Stamp. Void After June 30, 1947. U.S. Department of the Interior. $1."
Back: "It is unlawful to hunt waterfowl unless you sign your name in ink on the face of this stamp."
Plates Issued: 158448, 158449, 158456, 158457
Designer: William K. Schrage
1st Day of Sale: July 1, 1946
Qty. Sold: 2,016,841

Used			Unsigned			Mint		
AVG.	F	VF	NH F	NH VF	NH XF	H F	NH F	NH VF
$4	$12	$16	$10	$18	$20	$25	$28	$45

Price Guide & Collector's Log

1947 – 1948
Snow Geese
Artist: Jack Murray

#14

Front: "U.S. Department of the Interior. Void After June 30, 1948. Migratory Bird Hunting Stamp. $1."
Back: "It is unlawful to hunt waterfowl unless you sign your name in ink on the face of this stamp."
Plates Issued: 159461, 159462, 159463, 159464
Designer: Victor S. McCloskey, Jr.
1st Day of Sale: July 1, 1947
Qty. Sold: 1,722,677

Used			Unsigned			Mint		
AVG.	F	VF	NH F	NH VF	NH XF	H F	NH F	NH VF
$6	$13	$18	$12	$20	$22	$25	$28	$44

35

Price Guide & Collector's Log

This artist has five federal duck stamps to his credit.

1948 – 1949
Buffleheads
Artist: Maynard Reece

#15

Front: "U.S. Department of the Interior. Migratory Bird Hunting Stamp. Void After June 30, 1949. 1 Dollar."
Back: "It is unlawful to hunt waterfowl unless you sign your name in ink on the face of this stamp."
Plates Issued: 160099, 160100, 160101, 160102
Designer: Robert L. Miller, Jr.
1st Day of Sale: July 1, 1948
Qty. Sold: 2,127,603

Used		
AVG.	F	VF
$4	$12	$18

Unsigned		
NH F	NH VF	NH XF
$12	$20	$22

Mint		
H F	NH F	NH VF
$25	$35	$50

Price Guide & Collector's Log

First $2 stamp.

1949 – 1950
Common Goldeneyes
Artist: Roger E. Preuss

#16

Front: "Migratory Bird Hunting Stamp. U.S. Department of the Interior. Void After June 30, 1950. $2."
Back: "It is unlawful to hunt waterfowl unless you sign your name in ink on the face of this stamp."
Plates Issued: 160790, 160791, 160792, 160793
Designer: Robert L. Miller, Jr.
1st Day of Sale: September 1, 1949
Qty. Sold: 1,954,734

Used			Unsigned			Mint		
AVG.	F	VF	NH F	NH VF	NH XF	H F	NH F	NH VF
$4	$12	$18	$12	$21	$25	$30	$35	$55

37

Price Guide & Collector's Log

First year of the Federal Duck Stamp contest.

1950 – 1951
Trumpeter Swans
Artist: Walter A. Weber
#17

Front: "U.S. Department of the Interior. Void After June 30, 1951. Migratory Bird Hunting Stamp. $2."
Back: "It is unlawful to hunt waterfowl unless you sign your name in ink on the face of this stamp."
Plates Issued: 161533, 161534, 161535, 161536
Designer: Victor S. McCloskey, Jr.
1st Day of Sale: July 1, 1950
Qty. Sold: 1,903,644

Used		
AVG.	F	VF
$4	$8	$12

Unsigned		
NH F	NH VF	NH XF
$14	$21	$25

Mint		
H F	NH F	NH VF
$35	$45	$70

Price Guide & Collector's Log

1951 – 1952
Gadwalls
Artist: Maynard Reece

#18

Front: "U.S. Department of the Interior. Void After June 30, 1952. Migratory Bird Hunting Stamp. $2."
Back: "It is unlawful to hunt waterfowl unless you sign your name in ink on the face of this stamp."
Plates Issued: 162125, 162126, 162127, 162128
Designer: William K. Schrage
1st Day of Sale: July 1, 1951
Qty. Sold: 2,167,767

Used			*Unsigned*			*Mint*		
AVG.	F	VF	NH F	NH VF	NH XF	H F	NH F	NH VF
$4	$8	$12	$12	$21	$25	$35	$45	$70

Price Guide & Collector's Log

First stamp to include name of waterfowl species on front. Only issue to spell out "United States."

1952 – 1953
Harlequin Ducks
Artist: John H. Dick

#19

Front: "Migratory Bird Hunting Stamp. Harlequin Ducks. Void After June 30, 1953. 2 Dollars. U.S. Department of the Interior."
Back: "It is unlawful to hunt waterfowl unless you sign your name in ink on the face of this stamp."
Plates Issued: 162602, 162603, 162604, 162605
Designer: Robert L. Miller
1st Day of Sale: July 1, 1952
Qty. Sold: 2,296,628

Used

AVG.	F	VF
$4	$8	$12

Unsigned

NH F	NH VF	NH XF
$12	$24	$30

Mint

H F	NH F	NH VF
$35	$45	$70

Price Guide & Collector's Log

1953 – 1954
Blue-Winged Teal
Artist: Clayton B. Seagers

#20

Front: "Migratory Bird Hunting Stamp. 2 Dollars. Void After June 30, 1954. Blue-Winged Teal. U.S. Department of the Interior."
Back: "It is unlawful to hunt waterfowl unless you sign your name in ink on the face of this stamp."
Plates Issued: 163622, 163623, 163624, 163625
Designer: William K. Schrage
1st Day of Sale: July 1, 1953
Qty. Sold: 2,268,446

Used			Unsigned			Mint		
AVG.	F	VF	NH F	NH VF	NH XF	H F	NH F	NH VF
$4	$8	$12	$14	$24	$28	$35	$45	$80

Price Guide & Collector's Log

Only stamp with void after date twice on face.

1954 – 1955
Ring-Necked Duck
Artist: Harvey Dean Sandstrom

#21

Front: "Migratory Bird Hunting Stamp. Ring-Necked Duck. Void After June 30, 1955. $2. U.S. Department of Interior."
Back: "It is unlawful to hunt waterfowl unless you sign your name in ink on the face of this stamp."
Plates Issued: 164744, 164745, 164746, 164747
Designer: Victor S. McCloskey, Jr.
1st Day of Sale: July 1, 1954
Qty. Sold: 2,184,550

Used

AVG.	F	VF
$4	$8	$10

Unsigned

NH F	NH VF	NH XF
$14	$24	$28

Mint

H F	NH F	NH VF
$35	$45	$70

Price Guide & Collector's Log

1955 – 1956
Blue Geese
Artist: Stanley Stearns   **#22**

Front: "U.S. Department of the Interior. Void After June 30, 1956. Migratory Bird Hunting Stamp. $2. Blue Geese."
Back: "It is unlawful to hunt waterfowl unless you sign your name in ink on the face of this stamp."
Plates Issued: 165282, 165283, 165284, 165285
Designer: Robert J. Jones
1st Day of Sale: July 1, 1955
Qty. Sold: 2,369,940

Used			Unsigned			Mint		
AVG.	F	VF	NH F	NH VF	NH XF	H F	NH F	NH VF
$4	$8	$10	$14	$24	$28	$35	$45	$70

Price Guide & Collector's Log

1956 – 1957　　　　　　　　**#23**
American Merganser
Artist: Edward J. Bierly

Front: "U.S. Department of the Interior. Void After June 30, 1957. Migratory Bird Hunting Stamp. $2. American Merganser."
Back: "It is unlawful to hunt waterfowl unless you sign your name in ink on the face of this stamp."
Plates Issued: 165826, 165827, 165829, 165860
Designer: William K. Schrage
1st Day of Sale: July 1, 1956
Qty. Sold: 2,332,014

Used			Unsigned			Mint		
AVG.	F	VF	NH F	NH VF	NH XF	H F	NH F	NH VF
$4	$8	$10	$14	$24	$28	$35	$45	$75

44

Price Guide & Collector's Log

1957 – 1958
American Eider
Artist: Jackson Miles Abbott   **#24**

Front: "Migratory Bird Hunting Stamp. Void After June 30, 1958. $2. American Eider. U.S. Department of the Interior."
Back: "It is unlawful to hunt waterfowl unless you sign your name in ink on the face of this stamp."
Plates Issued: 166256, 166257, 166258, 166259
Designer: Victor S. McCloskey, Jr.
1st Day of Sale: July 1, 1957
Qty. Sold: 2,355,190

Used			Unsigned			Mint		
AVG.	F	VF	NH F	NH VF	NH XF	H F	NH F	NH VF
$4	$8	$10	$14	$24	$28	$35	$45	$75

45

Price Guide & Collector's Log

1958 – 1959 #25
Canada Geese
Artist: Leslie C. Louba

Front: "U.S. Department of the Interior. Void After June 30, 1959. Migratory Bird Hunting Stamp. $2. Canada Geese."
Back: "It is unlawful to hunt waterfowl unless you sign your name in ink on the face of this stamp."
Plates Issued: 166753, 166754, 166755, 166756
Designer: Robert L. Miller
1st Day of Sale: July 1, 1958
Qty. Sold: 2,176,425

Used		
AVG.	F	VF
$4	$8	$10

Unsigned		
NH F	NH VF	NH XF
$14	$24	$28

Mint		
H F	NH F	NH VF
$35	$45	$75

Price Guide & Collector's Log

First $3 stamp.
First issue to feature a theme.

1959 – 1960
Mallard with Labrador
Artist: Maynard Reece

#26

Front: "Migratory Bird Hunting Stamp. Retrievers Save Game. Void After June 30, 1960. $3. U.S. Department of the Interior."

Back: "Duck Stamps dollars buy wetlands to perpetuate waterfowl. It is unlawful to hunt waterfowl unless you sign your name in ink on the face of this stamp."

Plates Issued: 167109, 167120
Designer: Bob Hines & Victor S. McCloskey, Jr.
1st Day of Sale: July 1, 1959
Qty. Sold: 1,626,115

Used			Unsigned			Mint		
AVG.	F	VF	NH F	NH VF	NH XF	H F	NH F	NH VF
$4	$8	$14	$25	$35	$45	$60	$65	$85

47

Price Guide & Collector's Log

1960 – 1961
Redhead Ducks
#27
Artist: John A. Ruthven
Front: "U.S. Department of the Interior. Void After June 30, 1961. Migratory Bird Hunting Stamp. $3. Wildlife Needs Water.*Preserve Wetlands* Redhead Ducks."
Back: "Duck Stamps dollars buy wetlands to perpetuate waterfowl. It is unlawful to hunt waterfowl unless you sign your name in ink on the face of this stamp."
Plates Issued: 167498, 167503
Designer: Robert L. Miller
1st Day of Sale: July 1, 1960
Qty. Sold: 1,725.634

Used			Unsigned			Mint		
AVG.	F	VF	NH F	NH VF	NH XF	H F	NH F	NH VF
$4	$8	$12	$20	$32	$40	$50	$60	$75

Price Guide & Collector's Log

1961 – 1962
Mallard Brood
Artist: Edward A. Morris

#28

Front: "U.S. Department of the Interior. Void After June 30, 1962. Migratory Bird Hunting Stamp. $3. Mallard Brood, Habitat Produces Ducks."
Back: "Duck Stamps dollars buy wetlands to perpetuate waterfowl. It is unlawful to hunt waterfowl unless you sign your name in ink on the face of this stamp."
Plates Issued: 167768, 167772
Designer: Victor S. McCloskey, Jr.
1st Day of Sale: July 1, 1961
Qty. Sold: 1,334,236

Used			Unsigned			Mint		
AVG.	F	VF	NH F	NH VF	NH XF	H F	NH F	NH VF
$4	$8	$12	$25	$35	$40	$55	$65	$85

Price Guide & Collector's Log

1962 – 1963
Pintails   **#29**
Artist: Edward A. Morris

Front: "Pintails. U.S. Department of the Interior. Void After June 30, 1963. Migratory Bird Hunting Stamp. $3."
Back: "Duck Stamps dollars buy wetlands to perpetuate waterfowl. It is unlawful to hunt waterfowl unless you sign your name in ink on the face of this stamp."
Plates Issued: 168073
Designer: Robert L. Miller
1st Day of Sale: July 1, 1962
Qty. Sold: 1,147,212

Used			Unsigned			Mint		
AVG.	F	VF	NH F	NH VF	NH XF	H F	NH F	NH VF
$4	$8	$12	$30	$40	$45	$65	$70	$95

50

Price Guide & Collector's Log

1963 – 1964
Brant
Artist: Edward J. Bierly

#30

Front: "U.S. Department of the Interior. Void After June 30, 1964. Migratory Bird Hunting Stamp. $3. Brant."
Back: "Duck Stamps dollars buy wetlands to perpetuate waterfowl. It is unlawful to hunt waterfowl unless you sign your name in ink on the face of this stamp."
Plates Issued: 168269, 168273
Designer: William K. Schrage
1st Day of Sale: July 1, 1963
Qty. Sold: 1,448,191

Used			Unsigned			Mint		
AVG.	F	VF	NH F	NH VF	NH XF	H F	NH F	NH VF
$4	$8	$12	$36	$45	$50	$65	$70	$95

Price Guide & Collector's Log

1964 – 1965 #31
Nene Goose
Artist: Stanley Stearns
Front: "Migratory Bird Hunting Stamp. U.S. Department of the Interior. Void After June 30, 1965. $3. Nene Goose."
Back: "Duck Stamps dollars buy wetlands to perpetuate waterfowl. It is unlawful to hunt waterfowl unless you sign your name in ink on the face of this stamp."
Plates Issued: 168629, 168630
Designer: Robert L. Miller
1st Day of Sale: July 1, 1964
Qty. Sold: 1,573,155

Used			Unsigned			Mint		
AVG.	F	VF	NH F	NH VF	NH XF	H F	NH F	NH VF
$4	$8	$12	$35	$45	$50	$60	$65	$95

Price Guide & Collector's Log

First issue without a defined border.

1965 – 1966
Canvasbacks
Artist: Ron Jenkins

#32

Front: "Migratory Bird Hunting Stamp. Void After June 30, 1966. $3. Canvasbacks. U.S. Department of the Interior."
Back: "Duck Stamps dollars buy wetlands to perpetuate waterfowl. It is unlawful to hunt waterfowl unless you sign your name in ink on the face of this stamp."
Plates Issued: 168790, 168791
Designer: Robert L. Miller
1st Day of Sale: July 1, 1965
Qty. Sold: 1,558,197

Used			Unsigned			Mint		
AVG.	F	VF	NH F	NH VF	NH XF	H F	NH F	NH VF
$4	$10	$14	$35	$40	$45	$60	$65	$75

Price Guide & Collector's Log

1966 – 1967
Whistling Swans
Artist: Stanley Stearns

#33

Front: "Migratory Bird Hunting Stamp. U.S. Department of the Interior. Void After June 30, 1967. $3. Whistling Swans."
Back: "Duck Stamps dollars buy wetlands to perpetuate waterfowl. It is unlawful to hunt waterfowl unless you sign your name in ink on the face of this stamp."
Plates Issued: 169058, 169063
Designer: Howard C. Mildner
1st Day of Sale: July 1, 1966
Qty. Sold: 1,805,341

Used			Unsigned			Mint		
AVG.	F	VF	NH F	NH VF	NH XF	H F	NH F	NH VF
$4	$8	$12	$35	$45	$50	$65	$70	$95

Price Guide & Collector's Log

1967 – 1968   **#34**
Old Squaws
Artist: Leslie C. Kouba

Front: "Migratory Bird Hunting Stamp. $3. U.S. Department of the Interior. Void After June 30, 1968. Old Squaws."
Back: "Duck Stamps dollars buy wetlands to perpetuate waterfowl. It is unlawful to hunt waterfowl unless you sign your name in ink on the face of this stamp."
Plates Issued: 169457, 169487
Designer: Robert J. Jones
1st Day of Sale: July 1, 1967
Qty. Sold: 1,934,697

Used			Unsigned			Mint		
AVG.	F	VF	NH F	NH VF	NH XF	H F	NH F	NH VF
$4	$8	$10	$35	$40	$45	$60	$65	$110

Price Guide & Collector's Log

1968 – 1969
Hooded Mergansers
Artist: Claremont Gall Pritchard

#35

Front: "U.S. Department of the Interior. Void After June 30, 1969. Migratory Bird Hunting Stamp. $3. Hooded Mergansers."
Back: "Buy Duck Stamps. Save wetlands. Send in all bird bands. Sign your Duck Stamp."
Plates Issued: 170436, 170443
Designer: Leonard E. Buckley
1st Day of Sale: July 1, 1968
Qty. Sold: 1,837,139

Used			Unsigned			Mint		
AVG.	F	VF	NH F	NH VF	NH XF	H F	NH F	NH VF
$4	$8	$10	$15	$25	$28	$30	$45	$60

56

Price Guide & Collector's Log

1969 – 1970
White-Winged Scoters
Artist: Maynard Reece

#36

Front: "U.S. Department of the Interior. Void After June 30, 1970. Migratory Bird Hunting Stamp. $3. White-Winged Scoters."
Back: "Buy Duck Stamps. Save wetlands. Send in all bird bands. Sign your Duck Stamp."
Plates Issued: 170765, 170767
Designer: Howard C. Mildner
1st Day of Sale: July 1, 1969
Qty. Sold: 2,072,108

Used			Unsigned			Mint		
AVG.	F	VF	NH F	NH VF	NH XF	H F	NH F	NH VF
$4	$6	$9	$16	$22	$25	$32	$45	$55

57

Price Guide & Collector's Log

First intaglio/offset printed "Duck" stamp.

1970 – 1971
Ross' Geese
#37

Artist: Edward J. Bierly

Front: "Migratory Bird Hunting Stamp. Void After June 30, 1971. $3. Ross' Geese. U.S. Department of the Interior."
Back: "Buy Duck Stamps. Save wetlands. Send in all bird bands. It is unlawful to hunt waterfowl unless you sign your name in ink on the face of this stamp."
Plates Issued: 171165, 171169
Designer: Leonard E. Buckley
1st Day of Sale: July 1, 1970
Qty. Sold: 2,420,244

Used			Unsigned			Mint		
AVG.	F	VF	NH F	NH VF	NH XF	H F	NH F	NH VF
$4	$6	$8	$18	$25	$30	$35	$55	$65

Price Guide & Collector's Log

Highest sales of any issue.

1971 – 1972
Cinnamon Teal
Artist: Maynard Reece   **#38**

Front: "U.S. Department of the Interior. Void After June 30, 1972. Migratory Bird Hunting Stamp. $3. Cinnamon Teal."
Back: "Buy Duck Stamps. Save wetlands. Send in all bird bands. It is unlawful to hunt waterfowl unless you sign your name in ink on the face of this stamp."
Plates Issued: 171586, 171587
Designer: Leonard E. Buckley
1st Day of Sale: July 1, 1971
Qty. Sold: 2,445,977

Used			Unsigned			Mint		
AVG.	F	VF	NH F	NH VF	NH XF	H F	NH F	NH VF
$4	$6	$8	$14	$18	$20	$25	$30	$40

Price Guide & Collector's Log

First $5 stamp.

1972 – 1973
Emperor Geese
Artist: Arthur M. Cook

#39

Front: "U.S. Department of the Interior. Void After June 30, 1973. Migratory Bird Hunting Stamp. $5. Emperor Geese."
Back: "Buy Duck Stamps. Save wetlands. Send in all bird bands. Sign your Duck Stamp. It is unlawful to hunt waterfowl unless you sign your name in ink on the face of this stamp."
Plates Issued: 171862, 171864
Designer: Leonard E. Buckley
1st Day of Sale: July 1, 1972
Qty. Sold: 2,184,343

Used			Unsigned			Mint		
AVG.	F	VF	NH F	NH VF	NH XF	H F	NH F	NH VF
$4	$6	$8	$10	$12	$15	$16	$18	$25

Price Guide & Collector's Log

1973 – 1974
Steller's Eider
#40
Artist: Lee LeBlanc

Front: "U.S. Department of the Interior. Void After June 30, 1974. Migratory Bird Hunting Stamp. $5. Steller's Eider."
Back: "Buy Duck Stamps. Save wetlands. Send in all bird bands. Sign your Duck Stamp. It is unlawful to hunt waterfowl unless you sign your name in ink on the face of this stamp."
Plates Issued: 172101, 172102
Designer: Ronald C. Sharpe
1st Day of Sale: July 1, 1973
Qty. Sold: 2,094,414

Used

AVG.	F	VF
$4	$6	$8

Unsigned

NH F	NH VF	NH XF
$9	$10	$12

Mint

H F	NH F	NH VF
$15	$18	$25

Price Guide & Collector's Log

1974 – 1975   **#41**
Wood Duck
Artist: David A. Maass

Front: "U.S. Department of the Interior. Void After June 30, 1975. Migratory Bird Hunting Stamp. $5. Wood Duck."
Back: "Buy Duck Stamps. Save wetlands. Send in all bird bands. Sign your Duck Stamp. It is unlawful to hunt waterfowl unless you sign your name in ink on the face of this stamp."
Plates Issued: 172500, 172505
Designer: Frank J. Waslick
1st Day of Sale: July 1, 1974
Qty. Sold: 2,214,056

Used			Unsigned			Mint		
AVG.	F	VF	NH F	NH VF	NH XF	H F	NH F	NH VF
$3	$5	$7	$8	$9	$10	$12	$14	$18

Price Guide & Collector's Log

Only stamp to depict a decoy.

1975 – 1976
Canvasback
#42

Artist: James P. Fisher

Front: "U.S. Department of the Interior. Void After June 30, 1976. Migratory Bird Hunting Stamp. $5. Canvasback."

Back: "Buy Duck Stamps. Save wetlands. Send in all bird bands. Sign your Duck Stamp. It is unlawful to hunt waterfowl unless you sign your name in ink on the face of this stamp."

Plates Issued: 172775, 172777
Designer: V. Jack Ruther
1st Day of Sale: July 1, 1975
Qty. Sold: 2,237,126

Used			Unsigned			Mint		
AVG.	F	VF	NH F	NH VF	NH XF	H F	NH F	NH VF
$3	$5	$6	$7	$8	$9	$10	$12	$15

63

Price Guide & Collector's Log

1976 – 1977
Canada Geese
Artist: Alderson Magee

#43

Front: "U.S. Department of the Interior. Void After June 30, 1977. Migratory Bird Hunting Stamp. $5. Canada Geese."

Back: "Buy Duck Stamps. Save wetlands. Send in all bird bands. Sign your Duck Stamp. It is unlawful to hunt waterfowl unless you sign your name in ink on the face of this stamp."

Plates Issued: 173029, 173030
Designer: Peter Cocci
1st Day of Sale: July 1, 1976
Qty. Sold: 2,170,194

Used			Unsigned			Mint		
AVG.	F	VF	NH F	NH VF	NH XF	H F	NH F	NH VF
$3	$5	$6	$7	$8	$9	$10	$12	$15

Price Guide & Collector's Log

This year the wording on the stamp face was changed to include "and conservation."

1977 – 1978
Ross' Geese
Artist: Martin R. Murk

#44

Front: "U.S. Department of the Interior. Void After June 30, 1978. Migratory Bird Hunting and Conservation Stamp. $5. Ross' Geese."

Back: "Buy Duck Stamps. Save wetlands. Send in all bird bands. Sign your Duck Stamp. It is unlawful to hunt waterfowl unless you sign your name in ink on the face of this stamp."

Plates Issued: 173205, 173206
Designer: Esther Porter
1st Day of Sale: July 1, 1977
Qty. Sold: 2,196,774

Used			Unsigned			Mint		
AVG.	F	VF	NH F	NH VF	NH XF	H F	NH F	NH VF
$3	$5	$6	$7	$8	$9	$10	$12	$14

65

Price Guide & Collector's Log

First issue to show a single bird.

1978 – 1979
Hooded Merganser
Artist: Albert Earl Gilbert **#45**

Front: "U.S. Department of the Interior. Void After June 30, 1979. Migratory Bird Hunting and Conservation Stamp. $5. Hooded Merganser."
Back: "Buy Duck Stamps. Save wetlands. Send in all bird bands. Sign your Duck Stamp. It is unlawful to hunt waterfowl unless you sign your name in ink on the face of this stamp."
Plates Issued: 173331, 173333
Designer: Clarence Holbert
1st Day of Sale: July 1, 1978
Qty. Sold: 2,216,421

Used

AVG.	F	VF
$3	$5	$6

Unsigned

NH F	NH VF	NH XF
$7	$8	$9

Mint

H F	NH F	NH VF
$10	$12	$14

Price Guide & Collector's Log

First $7.50 stamp.

1979 – 1980
Green-Winged Teal
Artist: Lawrence K. Michaelson

#46

Front: "U.S. Department of the Interior. Void After June 30, 1980. Migratory Bird Hunting and Conservation Stamp. $7.50 Green-Winged Teal."
Back: "Buy Duck Stamps. Save wetlands. Send in all bird bands. Sign your Duck Stamp. It is unlawful to hunt waterfowl unless you sign your name in ink on the face of this stamp."
Plates Issued: 173422, 173423
Designer: Peter Cocci
1st Day of Sale: July 1, 1979
Qty. Sold: 2,090,155

Used			Unsigned			Mint		
AVG.	F	VF	NH F	NH VF	NH XF	H F	NH F	NH VF
$3	$5	$6	$7	$8	$9	$10	$12	$14

67

Price Guide & Collector's Log

1980 – 1981
Mallards
Artist: Richard W. Plasschaert

#47

Front: "U.S. Department of the Interior. Void After June 30, 1981. Migratory Bird Hunting and Conservation Stamp. $7.50. Mallards."
Back: "Buy Duck Stamps. Save wetlands. Send in all bird bands. Sign your Duck Stamp. It is unlawful to hunt waterfowl unless you sign your name in ink on the face of this stamp."
Plates Issued: 173492, 173493
Designer: V. Jack Ruther
1st Day of Sale: July 1, 1980
Qty. Sold: 2,045,114

Used			Unsigned			Mint		
AVG.	F	VF	NH F	NH VF	NH XF	H F	NH F	NH VF
$3	$5	$6	$7	$8	$9	$10	$12	$14

68

Price Guide & Collector's Log

1981 – 1982
Ruddy Ducks
Artist: John S. Wilson

#48

Front: "U.S. Department of the Interior. Void After June 30, 1982. Migratory Bird Hunting and Conservation Stamp. $7.50. Ruddy Ducks."
Back: "Buy Duck Stamps. Save wetlands. Send in all bird bands. Sign your Duck Stamp. It is unlawful to hunt waterfowl unless you sign your name in ink on the face of this stamp."
Plates Issued: 173572, 173573
Designer: Frank J. Waslick
1st Day of Sale: July 1, 1981
Qty. Sold: 1,907,120

Used			Unsigned			Mint		
AVG.	F	VF	NH F	NH VF	NH XF	H F	NH F	NH VF
$3	$5	$6	$7	$8	$10	$10	$12	$14

69

Price Guide & Collector's Log

1982 – 1983
Canvasbacks
Artist: David A. Maass

#49

Front: "U.S. Department of the Interior. Void After June 30, 1983. Migratory Bird Hunting and Conservation Stamp. $7.50. Canvasbacks."

Back: "Buy Duck Stamps. Save wetlands. Send in all bird bands. Sign your Duck Stamp. It is unlawful to hunt waterfowl unless you sign your name in ink on the face of this stamp."

Plates Issued: 173669, 173672
Designer: Ronald C. Sharpe
1st Day of Sale: July 1, 1982
Qty. Sold: 1,926,253

Used			Unsigned			Mint		
AVG.	F	VF	NH F	NH VF	NH XF	H F	NH F	NH VF
$3	$5	$6	$7	$8	$9	$10	$12	$14

Price Guide & Collector's Log

1983 – 1984
Pintails
Artist: Phil V. Scholer

#50

Front: "U.S. Department of the Interior. Void After June 30, 1984. Migratory Bird Hunting and Conservation Stamp. $7.50. Pintails."

Back: "Buy Duck Stamps. Save wetlands. Send in all bird bands. Sign your Duck Stamp. It is unlawful to hunt waterfowl unless you sign your name in ink on the face of this stamp."

Plates Issued: 173765, 173767
Designer: Clarence Holbert
1st Day of Sale: July 1, 1983
Qty. Sold: 1,867,998

Used			Unsigned			Mint		
AVG.	F	VF	NH F	NH VF	NH XF	H F	NH F	NH VF
$3	$5	$7	$8	$9	$10	$10	$12	$14

71

Price Guide & Collector's Log

50th Anniversary Stamp.

1984 – 1985
Wigeon
Artist: William C. Morris

#51

Front: "U.S. Department of the Interior. Void After June 30, 1985. Migratory Bird and Conservation Stamp. $7.50 Wigeon. 50th Anniversary 1934 – 1984."
Back: "Buy Duck Stamps. Save wetlands. Send in all bird bands. Sign your Duck Stamp. It is unlawful to hunt waterfowl unless you sign your name in ink on the face of this stamp."
Plates Issued: 173871, 172872, 173873, 173874
Designer: Ronald C. Sharpe
1st Day of Sale: July 2, 1984
Qty. Sold: 1,913,861

Used		
AVG.	F	VF
$3	$5	$7

Unsigned		
NH F	NH VF	NH XF
$8	$9	$10

Mint		
H F	NH F	NH VF
$12	$14	$16

Price Guide & Collector's Log

1985 – 1986
Cinnamon Teal
Artist: Gerald Mobley

#52

Front: "U.S. Department of the Interior. Void After June 30, 1986. Migratory Bird and Conservation Stamp. $7.50 Cinnamon Teal."

Back: "Buy Duck Stamps. Save wetlands. Send in all bird bands. Sign your Duck Stamp. It is unlawful to hunt waterfowl unless you sign your name in ink on the face of this stamp."

Plates Issued: 174343, 174350
Designer: V. Jack Ruther
1st Day of Sale: July 1, 1985
Qty. Sold: 1,780,636

Used			Unsigned			Mint		
AVG.	F	VF	NH F	NH VF	NH XF	H F	NH F	NH VF
$3	$5	$7	$8	$9	$10	$12	$14	$18

Price Guide & Collector's Log

1986 – 1987
Fulvous Whistling Duck
Artist: Burton E. Moore, Jr.

#53

Front: "U.S. Department of the Interior. Void After June 30, 1987. Migratory Bird and Conservation Stamp. $7.50 Fulvous Whistling Duck."

Back: "Buy Duck Stamps. Save wetlands. Send in all bird bands. Sign your Duck Stamp. It is unlawful to hunt waterfowl unless you sign your name in ink on the face of this stamp."

Plates Issued: 176844, 176845
Designer: Clarence Holbert
1st Day of Sale: July 1, 1986
Qty. Sold: 1,794,484

Used			Unsigned			Mint		
AVG.	F	VF	NH F	NH VF	NH XF	H F	NH F	NH VF
$3	$5	$6	$7	$8	$9	$10	$12	$14

Price Guide & Collector's Log

First $10 stamp. "The" was inadvertently omitted from left side.

1987 – 1988
Redhead Ducks
Artist: Arthur G. Anderson

#54

Front: "Migratory Bird Hunting and Conservation Stamp. Void After June 30, 1988. $10, Redhead Ducks, U.S. Department of Interior."

Back: "Take Pride in America, Buy Duck Stamps, Save Wetlands. Send in all bird bands. Sign your Duck Stamp. It is unlawful to hunt waterfowl unless you sign your name in ink on the face of this stamp."

Plates Issued: 178171 – 1
Designer: Esther Porter
1st Day of Sale: July 1, 1987
Qty. Sold: 1,663,470

Used			Unsigned			Mint		
AVG.	F	VF	NH F	NH VF	NH XF	H F	NH F	NH VF
$7	$8	$9	$9	$10	$12	$12	$15	$18

Price Guide & Collector's Log

1988 – 1989
Snow Goose
Artist: Daniel Smith

#55

Front: "Migratory Bird Hunting and Conservation Stamp. Void After June 30, 1989. $10, Snow Goose, U. S. Department of the Interior."
Back: "Take Pride in America, Buy Duck Stamps, Save Wetlands. Send in all bird bands. Sign your Duck Stamp. It is unlawful to hunt waterfowl unless you sign your name in ink on the face of this stamp."
Plates Issued: 180059 – 1
Designer: Frank J. Waslick
1st Day of Sale: July 1, 1988
Qty. Sold: 1,403,005

Used			Unsigned			Mint		
AVG.	F	VF	NH F	NH VF	NH XF	H F	NH F	NH VF
$7	$10	$12	$12	$15	$18	$20	$22	$25

Price Guide & Collector's Log

First $12.50 stamp.

1989 – 1990
Lesser Scaup
Artist: Neal R. Anderson

#56

Front: "Migratory Bird Hunting and Conservation Stamp. Void After June 30, 1990. $12.50. Lesser Scaup. U. S. Department of the Interior."
Back: "Take Pride in America, Buy Duck Stamps, Save Wetlands. Send in all bird bands. Sign your Duck Stamp. It is unlawful to hunt waterfowl unless you sign your name in ink on the face of this stamp."
Plates Issued: 182531
Designer: Ronald C. Sharpe
1st Day of Sale: July 1, 1989
Qty. Sold: 1,415,882

Used			Unsigned			Mint		
AVG.	F	VF	NH F	NH VF	NH XF	H F	NH F	NH VF
$7	$10	12	$12	$14	$16	$18	$20	$25

Price Guide & Collector's Log

1990 – 1991
Black Bellied Whistling Duck
Artist: Jim Hautman

#57

Front: "Migratory Bird Hunting and Conservation Stamp. Void After June 30, 1991. $12.50. Black Bellied Whistling Duck. U. S. Department of the Interior."
Back: "Take Pride in America. Buy Duck Stamps. Save Wetlands. Send in all bird bands. Sign your Duck Stamps. It is unlawful to hunt waterfowl or use this stamp as a National Wildlife entrance pass unless you sign your name in ink on the face of this stamp."
Plates Issued: 186360
Designer: Clarence Holbert
1st Day of Sale: June 30, 1990, Washington, DC; July 1, 1990, nationwide
Qty. Sold: 1,408,373

Used			*Unsigned*			*Mint*		
AVG.	F	VF	NH F	NH VF	NH XF	H F	NH F	NH VF
$7	$10	$12	$12	$14	$15	$16	$18	$22

Price Guide & Collector's Log

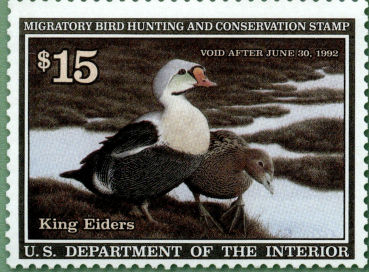

First $15.00 stamp.

1991 – 1992
King Eiders
#58

Artist: Nancy Howe (first selection of print by a woman)

Front: "Migratory Bird Hunting and Conservation Stamp. Void After June 30, 1992, $15. King Eiders. U. S. Department of the Interior."

Back: "Take Pride in America. Buy Duck Stamps. Save Wetlands. Send in all bird bands. It is unlawful to hunt waterfowl or use this stamp as a National Wildlife Refuge entrance pass unless you sign your name in ink on the face of this stamp."

Plates Issued: 188404
Designer: Peter Cocci
1st Day of Sale: June 30, 1991, Washington, DC; July 1, 1991, nationwide
Qty. Sold: 1,423,374

Used			Unsigned			Mint		
AVG.	F	VF	NH F	NH VF	NH XF	H F	NH F	NH VF
$8	$10	$12	$12	$14	$16	$18	$20	$25

Price Guide & Collector's Log

1992 – 1993
Spectacled Eider
Artist: Joseph Hautman

#59

Front: "Migratory Bird Hunting and Conservation Stamp. Void After June 30, 1993, $15. Spectacled Eider. U. S. Department of the Interior."
Back: "Take Pride in America. Buy Duck Stamps. Save Wetlands. Send in all bird bands. It is unlawful to hunt waterfowl or use this stamp as a National Wildlife Refuge entrance pass unless you sign your name in ink on the face of this stamp."
Plates Issued: 190493
Designer: Ronald C. Sharpe
1st Day of Sale: June 30, 1992, Washington, DC; July 1, 1992, nationwide
Qty. Sold: 1,347,393

Used			Unsigned			Mint		
AVG.	F	VF	NH F	NH VF	NH XF	H F	NH F	NH VF
$7	$9	$12	$12	$14	$16	$18	$20	$25

Price Guide & Collector's Log

1993 – 1994
Canvasbacks
Artist: Bruce Miller

#60

Front: "Migratory Bird Hunting and Conservation Stamp. Void After June 30, 1994, $15. Canvasbacks. U.S. Department of the Interior."
Back: "Take Pride in America. Buy Duck Stamps. Save Wetlands. Send in all bird bands. It is unlawful to hunt waterfowl or use this stamp as a National Wildlife Refuge entrance pass unless you sign your name in ink on the face of this stamp."
Plates Issued: 191659
Designer: V. Jack Ruther
1st Day of Sale: June 30, 1993, Washington, DC; July 1, 1993, nationwide
Qty. Sold: 1,402,569

Used			Unsigned			Mint		
AVG.	F	VF	NH F	NH VF	NH XF	H F	NH F	NH VF
$7	$9	$12	$12	$14	$16	$18	$20	$25

Price Guide & Collector's Log

1994 – 1995
Red-breasted Merganser
Artist: Neal Anderson

#61

Front: "Migratory Bird Hunting and Conservation Stamp. Void After June 30, 1995, $15. Red-breasted Merganser. U.S. Department of the Interior."

Back: "Invest in America's future. Buy Duck Stamps. Save Wetlands. Send in all bird bands. It is unlawful to hunt waterfowl or use this stamp as a pass to a National Wildlife Refuge unless you sign your name in ink on the face of this stamp."

Plates Issued: 193700
Designer: V. Jack Ruther
1st Day of Sale: June 30, 1994, Washington, DC; July 1, 1994, nationwide
Qty. Sold: 1,471,751

Used			Unsigned			Mint		
AVG.	F	VF	NH F	NH VF	NH XF	H F	NH F	NH VF
$7	$9	$12	$12	$14	$16	$18	$20	$25

Price Guide & Collector's Log

1995 – 1996
Mallards
Artist: Jim Hautman

#62

Front: "Migratory Bird Hunting and Conservation Stamp. Void After June 30, 1996, $15. Mallards. U.S. Department of the Interior."
Back: "Invest in America's Future. Buy Duck Stamps. Save Wetlands. Send in all bird bands. It is unlawful to hunt waterfowl or use this stamp as a pass to a National Wildlife Refuge unless you sign your name in ink on the face of this stamp."
Plates Issued: 195213
Designer: John Murray
1st Day of Sale: June 30, 1995, Washington, DC; July 1, 1995, nationwide
Qty. Sold: 1,539,622

Used			Unsigned			Mint		
AVG.	F	VF	NH F	NH VF	NH XF	H F	NH F	NH VF
$7	$9	$12	$12	$14	$16	$18	$20	$25

Price Guide & Collector's Log

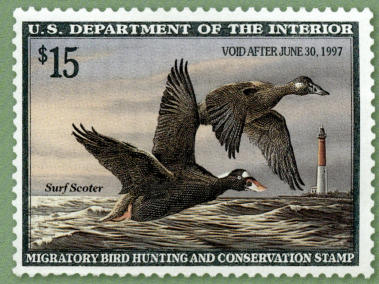

1996 – 1997
Surf Scoter
Artist: Wilhelm Goebel

#63

Front: "Migratory Bird Hunting and Conservation Stamp. Void After June 30, 1997, $15. Surf Scoter. U.S. Department of the Interior."
Back: "Invest in America's Future. Buy Duck Stamps. Save Wetlands. Send in all bird bands. It is unlawful to hunt waterfowl or use this stamp as a pass to a National Wildlife Refuge unless you sign your name in ink on the face of this stamp."
Plates Issued: 195744
Designer: Brian Thompson
1st Day of Sale: June 27, 1996, Washington, DC ; July 1, 1996, nationwide
Qty. Sold: 1,559,093

Used			Unsigned			Mint		
AVG.	F	VF	NH F	NH VF	NH XF	H F	NH F	NH VF
$7	$9	$12	$12	$14	$16	$18	$20	$25

Price Guide & Collector's Log

1997 – 1998
Canada Goose
Artist: Robert Hautman

#64

Front: "Migratory Bird Hunting and Conservation Stamp. Void After June 30, 1998, $15. Canada Goose. U.S. Department of the Interior."

Back: "Invest in America's Future. Buy Duck Stamps. Save Wetlands. (Added this year) Send in or report all bird bands to 1-800-327-BAND. It is unlawful to hunt waterfowl or use this stamp as a pass to a National Wildlife Refuge unless you sign your name in ink on the face of this stamp."

Plates Issued: 196441
Designer: Peter Cocci
1st Day of Sale: June 21, 1997, McLean, VA (only); July 1, 1997, nationwide
Qty. Sold: 1,696,513

Used			Unsigned			Mint		
AVG	F	VF	NH F	NH VF	NH XF	H F	NH F	NH VF
$7	$9	$12	$12	$14	$16	$18	$20	$25

Price Guide & Collector's Log

1998 – 1999
Barrow's Goldeneye
Artist: Robert Steiner

#65

Front: "Migratory Bird Hunting and Conservation Stamp. Void After June 30, 1999, $15. Barrow's Goldeneye U.S. Department of the Interior."

Back: "Invest in America's Future. Buy Duck Stamps. Save Wetlands. Send in or report all bird bands to 1-800-327-BAND. It is unlawful to hunt waterfowl or use this stamp as a pass to a National Wildlife Refuge unless you sign your name in ink on the face of this stamp."

Plates Issued: 197573
Designer: Peter Cocci
1st Day of Sale: July 1, 1998, Washington, DC
1st Self-Adhesive Issue: #65SA
Qty. Sold: 1,627,521

Used			Unsigned			Mint		
AVG.	F	VF	NH F	NH VF	NH XF	H F	NH F	NH VF
$7	$9	$12	$12	$14	$16	$18	$20	$25

Price Guide & Collector's Log

1999 – 2000
Greater Scaup
Artist: Jim Hautman

#66

Front: "Migratory Bird Hunting and Conservation Stamp. Void After June 30, 2000, $15. Greater Scaup, U.S. Department of the Interior."

Back: "Invest in America's Future. Buy Duck Stamps. Save Wetlands. Send in or report all bird bands to 1-800-327-BAND. It is unlawful to hunt waterfowl or use this stamp as a pass to a National Wildlife Refuge unless you sign your name in ink on the face of this stamp."

Plates Issued: 198656
Designer: Brian Thompson
1st Day of Sale: July 1, 1999, Washington, DC
Second Self-Adhesive Issue: #66SA
Qty. Sold: 1,600,000+

Used			Unsigned			Mint		
AVG	F	VF	NH F	NH VF	NH XF	H F	NH F	NH VF
$7	$9	$12	$12	$14	$16	$18	$20	$25

87

Price Guide & Collector's Log

2000 – 2001
Mottled Duck
Artist: Adam Grimm (at age 21, youngest artist to win contest)

#67

Front: "U.S. Department of the Interior. Migratory Bird Hunting and Conservation Stamp. Void After June 30, 2001, $15. Mottled Duck."

Back: "Invest in America's Future. Buy Duck Stamps And Save Wetlands. Send in or report all bird bands to 1-800-327-BAND. It is unlawful to hunt waterfowl or use this stamp as a pass to a National Wildlife Refuge unless you sign your name in ink on the face of this stamp."

Designer: Brian Thompson
1st Day of Sale: July 1, 2000, Washington, DC
Self-Adhesive Issue: #67SA
Qty. Sold: 1,600,000+

Used			Unsigned			Mint		
AVG.	F	VF	NH F	NH VF	NH XF	H F	NH F	NH VF
$6	$8	$10	$12	$14	$16	$18	$20	$25

Price Guide & Collector's Log

2001 – 2002
Northern Pintail
Artist: Robert Hautman

#68

Front: "U.S. Department of the Interior. Migratory Bird Hunting and Conservation Stamp. Void After June 30, 2002. $15. Northern Pintail."

Back: "Invest in America's Future. Buy Duck Stamps And Save Wetlands. Send in or report all bird bands to 1-800-327-BAND. It is unlawful to hunt waterfowl or use this stamp as a pass to a National Wildlife Refuge unless you sign your name in ink on the face of this stamp."

Plates Issued: 199121
Designer: Brian Thompson
1st Day of Sale: July 1, 2001, Washington, DC
Self-Adhesive Issue: #68SA
Qty. Sold: 1,600,000+

Used			Unsigned			Mint		
AVG.	F	VF	NH F	NH VF	NH XF	H F	NH F	NH VF
$6	$8	$10	$12	$14	$16	$18	$20	$25

89

Resources

These excellent resources will help you add to your collections as well as provide supplies, licenses, and other related products. Although we recommend these individuals and organizations, we do not represent them nor should we be held responsible for any losses that you may incur when dealing with them.

ORGANIZATIONS

Federal Duck Stamp Program
1849 C Street, NW Suite 2058
Washington, DC 20240
Phone: 202-208-4354
Fax: 202-208-6296
Bob Lesino, Chief, DSO
E-mail: robert_lesino@fws.gov
To order Federal Duckstamps or Junior Duckstamps by mail, call 1-877-887-5508.
Be sure to check out their informative website: www.duckstamps.fws.gov

National Duck Stamp Collectors Society
P. O. Box 43
Harleysville, PA 19438-0043
www.hwcn.org/link/ndscs
To promote and encourage collecting of migratory waterfowl hunting and conservation stamps.

American Philatelic Society
P. O. Box 8000
State College, PA 16803
Phone: 814-237-3803
www.stamps.org
Founded in 1886, the largest non-profit society for stamp collectors.

DEALERS

Brookman Stamps
Michael Jaffe Stamps, Inc
P.O.Box 61484
Vancouver, WA 98666-1484
Phone: 360-695-6161
www.brookmanstamps.com

National Wildlife Philatelics
11000-31 Metro Parkway
Fort Myers, Florida 33912-1293
Phone: 1-941-275-0500
Fax: 1-941-936-2788
E-mail: stamps@nationalwildlife.com
Website: www.nationalwildlife.com

Sam Houston Duck Co.
A division of Sam Houston Philatelics
P. O. Box 820087
Houston, TX 77282
Phone: 800-231-5926, 281-493-6386
www.shduck.com

Trenton Stamp and Coin
P. O. Box 8574
Trenton, NJ 08650
Phone: 609-584-8100

Resources

PUBLICATIONS

The Duck Stamp Story: Art, Conservation, History
by Bob Dumaine and Eric J. Dolin
Krause Publications, copyright 2000

2002 Krause-Minkus Standard Catalog of U.S. Stamps, 5th Edition
Maurice D. Wozniak, Editor
Krause Publications, copyright 2001

Linn's Stamp News
P.O. Box 29
Sidney, OH 45365
website: www.linns.com
A weekly newspaper that often features columns by Bob Dumaine, a national authority on duck stamps. Their website is also a great resource for all stamp collectors.

Scott Stamp Monthly
Scott Publishing Company
P.O. Box 828
Sidney, OH 45365
www.scottonline.com
The Scott Specialized Catalog is devoted to Duck Stamps. A great source for collector's supplies.

EXHIBITS

"Artistic License: The Duck Stamp Story"
National Postal Museum/Smithsonian Institution
Washington, DC
Showcases the artistry and history of Migratory Hunting Stamps. Well worth the trip!

WEBSITES

Stamp Sites
www.stampsites.com
The search engine for stamp collectors.

Stamp Dealers
www.stampdealers.com
Features dealers and classified ads for stamps.

Ding Darling Wildlife Society
www.dingdarlingsociety.org
Nonprofit association preserving the wildlife and habitat in the J.N. Ding Darling National Wildlife Refuge on Sanibel Island, Florida.

The Nature Conservancy
www.nature.org

Delta Waterfowl
www.deltawaterfowl.org

Ducks Unlimited
www.ducks.org

Reference List

This handy reference list serves as an index but can also be used to record your collection. Just put a check in each box as you acquire that stamp issue. This checklist will show at a glance how many you've got and those you still need!

Page

- [ ] #1 (1934 – 1935) Mallards 22
- [ ] #2 (1935 – 1936) Canvasbacks 23
- [ ] #3 (1936 – 1937) Canada Geese 24
- [ ] #4 (1937 – 1938) Greater Scaups 25
- [ ] #5 (1938 – 1939) Northern Pintails 26
- [ ] #6 (1939 – 1940) Green-Winged Teal 27
- [ ] #7 (1940 – 1941) Black Ducks 28
- [ ] #8 (1941 – 1942) Ruddy Ducks 29
- [ ] #9 (1942 – 1943) American Wigeons 30
- [ ] #10 (1943 – 1944) Wood Ducks 31
- [ ] #11 (1944 – 1945) White-Fronted Geese 32
- [ ] #12 (1945 – 1946) Northern Shovelers 33
- [ ] #13 (1946 – 1947) Redheads 34
- [ ] #14 (1947 – 1948) Snow Geese 35
- [ ] #15 (1948 – 1949) Buffleheads 36
- [ ] #16 (1949 – 1950) Common Goldeneyes 37

Reference List

	Page
☐ #17 (1950 – 1951) Trumpeter Swans	38
☐ #18 (1951 – 1952) Gadwalls	39
☐ #19 (1952 – 1953) Harlequin Ducks	40
☐ #20 (1953 – 1954) Blue-Winged Teal	41
☐ #21 (1954 – 1955) Ring-Necked Duck	42
☐ #22 (1955 – 1956) Blue Geese	43
☐ #23 (1956 – 1957) American Merganser	44
☐ #24 (1957 – 1958) American Eider	45
☐ #25 (1958 – 1959) Canada Geese	46
☐ #26 (1959 – 1960) Mallard with Labrador	47
☐ #27 (1960 – 1961) Redhead Ducks	48
☐ #28 (1961 – 1962) Mallard Brood	49
☐ #29 (1962 – 1963) Pintails	50
☐ #30 (1963 – 1964) Brant	51
☐ #31 (1964 – 1965) Nene Goose	52
☐ #32 (1965 – 1966) Canvasbacks	53
☐ #33 (1966 – 1967) Whistling Swans	54
☐ #34 (1967 – 1968) Old Squaws	55
☐ #35 (1968 – 1969) Hooded Mergansers	56
☐ #36 (1969 – 1970) White-Winged Scoters	57

Reference List

	Page
☐ #37 (1970 – 1971) Ross' Geese	58
☐ #38 (1971 – 1972) Cinnamon Teal	59
☐ #39 (1972 – 1973) Emperor Geese	60
☐ #40 (1973 – 1974) Steller's Eider	61
☐ #41 (1974 – 1975) Wood Duck	62
☐ #42 (1975 – 1976) Canvasback	63
☐ #43 (1976 – 1977) Canada Geese	64
☐ #44 (1977 – 1978) Ross' Geese	65
☐ #45 (1978 – 1979) Hooded Merganser	66
☐ #46 (1979 – 1980) Green-Winged Teal	67
☐ #47 (1980 – 1981) Mallards	68
☐ #48 (1981 – 1982) Ruddy Ducks	69
☐ #49 (1982 – 1983) Canvasbacks	70
☐ #50 (1983 – 1984) Pintails	71
☐ #51 (1984 – 1985) Wigeon	72
☐ #52 (1985 – 1986) Cinnamon Teal	73
☐ #53 (1986 – 1987) Fulvous Whistling Duck	74
☐ #54 (1987 – 1988) Redhead Ducks	75
☐ #55 (1988 – 1989) Snow Goose	76
☐ #56 (1989 – 1990) Lesser Scaup	77
☐ #57 (1990 – 1991) Black Bellied Whistling Duck	78

Reference List

	Page
☐ #58 (1991 – 1992) King Eiders	79
☐ #59 (1992 – 1993) Spectacled Eider	80
☐ #60 (1993 – 1994) Canvasbacks	81
☐ #61 (1994 – 1995) Red-breasted Merganser	82
☐ #62 (1995 – 1996) Mallards	83
☐ #63 (1996 – 1997) Surf Scoter	84
☐ #64 (1997 – 1998) Canada Goose	85
☐ #65 (1998 – 1999) Barrow's Goldeneye	86
☐ #66 (1999 – 2000) Greater Scaup	87
☐ #67 (2000 – 2001) Mottled Duck	88
☐ #68 (2001 – 2002) Northern Pintail	89

Hook one of these!

The Heddon Legacy, A Century of Classic Lures
Bill Roberts & Rob Pavey

This book has more than 1,100 color photographs illustrating Heddon's rise to prominence in the early years and its domination of the American tackle market well into the 1950s. There is also a complete photo reference of the most valuable Heddon lures, and an extensive, never-before-seen section on Heddon advertising pieces and one-of-a-kind lures and memorabilia.

ISBN: 1-57432-251-6 • #5912 • 8½ x 11 • 384 Pgs. • HB • $29.95

Fishing Lure Collectibles, 2nd Edition
Dudley Murphy & Rick Edmisten

This second edition contains hundreds of full-color photos and chapters on the "big ten" companies, miscellaneous companies, metal lures, handmade lures, and the seldom-seen experimental lures. Emphasizing antique lures made before 1940, this deluxe book contains over 1,300 lures beautifully reproduced in full color. With descriptions, sizes, dates, and current values.

ISBN: 1-57432-196-X • #5683 • 8½ x 11 • 400 Pgs. • HB • $29.95

Collector's Encyclopedia of Creek Chub Lures & Collectibles, 2nd Edition
Harold E. Smith, M.D.

This second edition of the *Collector's Encyclopedia of Creek Chub Lures* showcases these remarkable lures and contains over 1,100 full-color photographs, depicting every type of lure ever produced by the company. Plus there are many other fishing collectibles featured, as well as charts, historical pictures, and catalogs.

ISBN: 1-57432-245-1 • #5906 • 8½ x 11 • 304 Pgs. • HB • $29.95

1-800-626-5420
www.collectorbooks.com